GOD IN MY EVERYDAY

Books by Flora Larsson

JUST A MOMENT, LORD
MY BEST MEN ARE WOMEN
BETWEEN YOU AND ME, LORD
TOWARDS YOU LORD

GOD
IN MY EVERYDAY

FLORA LARSSON

HODDER AND STOUGHTON
LONDON   SYDNEY   AUCKLAND   TORONTO

British Library Cataloguing in Publication Data

Larsson, Flora
   God in my everyday.———(Hodder Christian paperback)
   1. Christian LIFE
   i. title
   248.4   BV4501.2

   ISBN 0-340-34642-6

Printed in Great Britain for Hodder and Stoughton Limited, Mill Road, Dunton Green, Sevenoaks, Kent by Hunt Barnard Printing Ltd, Aylesbury, Bucks.

Photoset by Rowland Phototypesetting Ltd, Bury St Edmunds, Suffolk.
Hodder and Stoughton Editorial Office: 47 Bedford Square, London WC1B 3DP.

CONTENTS

GOD AND MYSELF

GOD IN MY STRIVINGS

GOD FOR ALL SEASONS

GOD IN MY JOYS

Home

I look around my little paradise
      and thank You for my home, Lord.
It is not lavishly equipped,
but it is the welcome shell
into which my tired body and frayed soul
      creep at end of working day,
or quite simply after a bout of shopping!

The well-used furniture stores memories
      of many events
as well as the pleasant routine
      of evenly passing hours.
A few photos greet me cheerily . . .
      family and friends
      caught in a set pose
but remembered as lively individuals.

Warm, comforting place . . . my home.
I am glad that I can welcome You there, Master.
My somewhat envious thoughts turn to the times
      You shared meals with Your friends
      In Palestine.
Homely fare in a homely atmosphere . . .
      a broken loaf, a piece of fish
      and pleasant, intimate talk.
Be my guest, Master!
Let my door always be open to Your knock.

Too much

I feel I have too much, Lord!
      Too much of good things.
Out of the pale blue sky the sun shines
      through my windows,
while frost crystals sparkle on the grass.
A pleasant warmth surrounds me indoors.
I am well clad to maintain comfort
      and to save energy
which for most of us means to save expense!

I raise my heart to You in thanksgiving
when suddenly this feeling of 'too much'
      overwhelms me.

Yes, I have had my troubles and my sorrows,
     my problems and my pains,
but just now all is well. I am at peace
     within and without.
It almost seems *too much!*

I make that feeling the basis of my prayer.
     Thank You, Lord,
     thank You for everything.
Grant that the smooth tenor of my present lot
may lead me nearer You in deep gratitude,
and may my heart be more open to those
     less fortunate than I.

Golden spring

O God, how liberally You clothe the world in yellow,
     particularly in spring!
After winter's greyness and chill
You brush Your yellow tones over the drab country-
     side,
     in blazing points of golden light.
How beautiful is Your world in springtime!

Coltsfoot flowers hug the brown earth closely,
      as yet unshielded by leaves.
Forsythia decorates the bushes while daffodils
      flaunt their trumpets in the breeze,
and dandelions peep cheekily up from the grass.
Over the moors the gorse flames into colour
while pale primroses cuddle shyly near the hedges.
Breathtakingly lovely is Your world!

Parting the clouds the sun emerges
      bolder for every day;
the golden sunlight filters through in cascades
      of shining warmth.
How my heart responds to springtime, Lord!
Not only do all my senses rejoice
      but in my heart there is
      a golden ray of new hope,
      kindly by Your love.
Winter is past; my flagging spirits revive.
I am conscious of Your nearness . . .
      Thank You, Lord.

Friendship

You, Master, knew the worth of friends
    and drew them close to You.
From Your seventy-two evangelists
    You chose twelve disciples;
From those twelve an inner circle of three
and from that trio one special friend
    closer to Your heart and mind
    than any of the others.
The strength of it! To have a human face,
    a human voice and heart
reaching out in staunch support.

So You understand our need of friends
and our pleasure when we find them.
Help us to treasure the bond of friendship,
treating it as a precious privilege
    to be used but not abused.
Let us not be demanding of time,
    interest or involvement.
Preserve us from thinking that we own our friends,
    or that they owe us something.
Let us not stretch the links between us
    to breaking point.

Thank You, Lord, for friends
      past and present.
Above all, for Your companionship.

Enjoyment

Today, Master, I will enjoy Your world.
Many times I wander through the hours
      busy with this and that
but not absorbing my surroundings.
Today is going to be different!
Today I pledge myself to enjoy
      colour and tone
      sound and smell
      light and shade
      taste and touch
      shape and texture.
What a lot of good things this old world holds!

Deepen my awareness, Lord!
Let me respond more readily to my environment.
Let me see with new appreciation,
hear with more intent listening,
taste, savouring with my tongue,
feel with sensitised fingers
      the angular, the curved,
      the rough, the smooth.

Why! even one room can become
        an exciting place to explore
if I use all my sharpened senses.

I will rest in Your joyous presence, Lord.
Safe in the shelter of Your love
        I will enjoy Your world
with all its delights and surprises.

Let there be grass

Let there be grass in heaven, Lord!
My awakened eyes might weary
        of the constant gleam of gold,
and long for earth's cool greening places,
its gardens, moors and meadows.

I've lived in the snowy north
        where all was whiteness,
tiring to the eyes without due protection
but pleasant to the aesthetic sense . . .
diamond glint of frost crystals,
gorgeous blazings of sunrise and sunset,
or purple-blue shadows lengthening on snow wastes.

I've lived in the torrid south
with every green blade scorched from the earth
    for the summer months.
An arid, desert landscape,
life sucked from it for a season
    until rain again fell.
Hot sunshine every day can become tedious.

So I beg You, Master,
    let there be grass in heaven!
Grass where small cherubs roll and tumble,
    tired of flying,
and where more mature angels can sit and chat,
or gently twang their harps and sing.
Please, Lord, let there be grass in heaven,
even if I have to mow it myself.

Someone to thank

Whatever should I do, Master,
    if I had no one to thank;
no one to whom I could look up and say,
    gratefully and happily,
      'Thank You, Lord'?
You, the Author of all good,
Creator of all beauty and love!

How often my heart lifts to You
      on quite an ordinary day.
It keeps the link between us vital and maintains
      the atmosphere of trust.
How deprived I should feel if I didn't know You
      well enough to say:
      'Thank You, Lord'
at least a dozen times a day.

Thanks for each new day that dawns,
      for eyes to see
      and ears to hear,
for limbs that move at my behest.
Thanks for all the lovely things this old earth holds
      for pleasure and enrichment.
Then the grateful stretching out in bed
      when night-time falls,
a last swift prayer into Your ear
      before I slumber:
      'Thank You, Lord'.

This beautiful planet

This beautiful planet, hanging in space
      like a precious jewel
      lit by solar light
      to be admired.

Its icecaps shining brilliantly,
      its continents and seas defined,
so wondrous, so pure, so perfect . . .
This planet earth – my home.

But come nearer and see the zealously guarded frontiers
      the rocket ranges and bomber planes
      the armoury of nuclear weapons,
      high fences and barbed wire.
Come nearer still and notice
      the pollution of rivers and seas,
the smoking chimneys spewing out poisonous waste,
the great flecks of crude oil on the oceans;
and ever nearer . . .
      political rivalries
      race discrimination
      divided homes
      unwanted children.

O beautiful planet . . . my home . . . *our* home,
What can we do to save you from self-destruction?
      O God, in Your mercy
      grant us wisdom
      and understanding
      . . . and love.

GOD IN MY QUIET
TIMES

My visiting list

My visiting list is restricted, Master.
      It might be called selective.
There are family calls, friendly calls and duty visits
      when people are ill or in trouble.
But *You* are also on my list, Lord.
I call at Your House each Sunday morning,
      hoping to find You in.
I dress especially for the occasion
      in my best clothes
      and I always go prepared to listen
      to what You have to say,
although I rarely receive any direct message.

In addition I am 'at home' to You
      each morning after breakfast
      for a set time,
when I read Your Book, meditate and pray.
If I fail in this I feel I must apologise to You.

So what is missing, Master? Isn't this enough?
     What more can You expect?
Why should my heart feel cold when I have such a
     good working programme with You?
Ah! I know the answer, Lord.
These splendid commitments are but the externals,
     the cool technique, the duty run.
What You desire is the loving look,
     the quick lifting of the heart
     at any moment of the day . . .
to thank, to praise or to worship mutely.
I have kept the outward form without the strong intent.
     Pardon me, Lord!
Let me not give You less time but rather put more
     ardour
     into my search for You
and Your companionship in my every day.

Credit cards

Credit cards are in fashion, Lord.
Everyone must own at least one
     to be accepted at face value,
a guarantee of money to be paid later.
It is so easy and such a sop to pride!

TV advertisements make it look alluring.
You flourish your card – the waiter bows,
    the bank manager smiles,
    the salesman nods respectfully.
A credit card gives access to the best
    this world can offer.

What have we, Master, to commend ourselves to You?
    To ensure the open door to Your presence
and usher us into the awesome majesty of God?
Here no earthly credit card avails
however much wealth it represents.

But Your Book tells us that through You, O Christ,
    we have access to God
to whom we can come with confidence.
    What a privilege!
    What a priceless possession,
the invisible though real access card gaining us,
    not only entrance,
but a welcome and a hearing when we come
    with our needs to God.

God-moments

Lord, teach me to make brief pauses
      in the rhythm of my days,
to quiet my mind, relax my muscles
      and rest my soul.
Life is so wearing!
      So continual and persistent.
The minutes trudge on mechanical feet
      throughout the hours,
pacing out the passage of time
      with unrelenting doom.
At times I gasp for a space,
      a pause in the steady pressure,
but then I realise, Master, that only I
      can create brief breaks
in the monotony of routine.

So I ask for Your help, Lord.
Teach me to make pauses,
      brief but effective breaks
      for God-moments.
A winged prayer for Your blessing,
      murmured thanks for Your love,
      a swift uplook into Your face,
a nestling into Your tender care.

There will be no chance for more
While duties demand their toll of time,
      but this small sacred oasis
      will refresh my heart
and keep me close to You.
Master, teach me the value of God-moments
      throughout my day.

Becoming rich

Lord, today I ponder some wise words:
There are two ways of becoming rich . . .
      to amass possessions
      or to reduce your wants.
The first is closed to me.
Thank You for the common sense which tells me that!
But the second is open . . .
      to reduce my actual needs,
      to see what I can do without
and still live happily.

It can be fun, Lord,
      a kind of permanent challenge
      to a simpler life-style,
checking up on what I have

before acquiring more.
Making over, re-styling, making do
      as in wartime economies.

Fortunately I have ceased growing upwards
and I am careful not to grow outward
      by putting on weight.
So my clothes last a long time
      and that is all to the good.
None of this will give me a larger bank balance
but it will give me serenity of mind
      and health of body,
and that is one way of becoming rich.

Family

How good to be part of a family, Lord!
      To *belong* to a related group.
You had Your brothers and sisters around You
      in the home of Nazareth
so You know something of the give and take,
      the friendly rivalry
      yet deep loyalty
      of family bonds.

The closeness of it! The strength in belonging,
    of having a base
    a safe anchorage
    a home port,
different from all other places of call.

Thank You, Master, for my family,
embracing blood-ties, in-laws
    and cousins of all grades.
How many there must be I have never counted.
Because of my wandering life only a few
    are known to me personally,
yet we all belong in a loosely-woven web
    of relationship.

My prayer today, Lord, is for those without family;
The very old who have outlived their relatives,
refugees who have lost contact with their own,
    the many-times bereaved,
the lonely souls with a wind-swept space around them.
Be to them, Master, a close Friend, a Father,
taking away some of their isolation.

Silence

How difficult it is, Lord,
to achieve a few moments of silence.
This noisy world presses upon our senses.
Even if we shut off TV and radio in our home
      we hear the distant hum of traffic
       and the vibration of planes overhead.
Some people are so attuned to noise that they
      shun silence as ominous,
whereas it has a healing virtue all its own.

I remember, Master, how You loved
      the silence of the hills
where You withdrew in solitude for prayer.
It was easier in Your days on earth
      to reach open country.
Today our towns spread out like ugly growths
swallowing up green fields and hedges.
For us the solitude of hills becomes
      just a picture on a postcard
or a painting hung on our wall.
Our imagination must place us in the scene.
The silence is perhaps only a few moments
      at dawn or dusk
or stolen between duties.

Help me, Lord, however difficult my circumstances,
to make some brief break of silence daily,
      when I quiet myself before You,
think of Your peace stealing into my heart,
rest in Your love and rejoice in Your goodness,
        without uttering a word.
You will be there and know how to meet my need.

On the sidelines

I've been transferred to the sidelines, Master!
No more for me the taxing schedule,
      the demanding duties,
      the heavy pressures.
I have been thanked for past service
(and how well my record was made to sound!)
Then I was duly retired, so now
      I stand on the sidelines,
watching the surgings of the game of life.

It was a great relief, Lord, at first . . .
to relax, call time my own;
      to plan or not to plan
      to go out or stay in
      just as I wished.

Then came a feeling of emptiness,
of something lacking.
To think that one could become
weary of resting!

How shall I fill up time, Master?
Shall I fill it like a Christmas stocking
with lots of goodies and small delights?
Or shall I heroically choose a demanding course,
a complicated hobby
or some social involvement?
You must help me to decide aright, Lord,
for the years of my life which lie ahead
might be many,
and I would not have them
worthlessly frittered away.

Silent heroism

Master, I deeply admire such people!
They seldom make news headlines but the silent
heroism
of their daily lives
brings a warmth of benediction to my heart.

I think of a woman I know
        caring for her husband at home,
lovingly tending his frail body and
sadly bearing with his failing mind.
It is a triumph of enduring love,
        breath-taking in its scope.

I remember a mother with a handicapped child,
not counting the bonds of duty a prison
        but nobly accepting
the surrender of personal freedom.

Such love is like Your love, Lord,
        enduring, outliving
        all rational limits.
It is a portion of divine love sliced from
        Your abundant supply . . .
a love that is increased by the very demands
        made upon it,
rather than diminished by the costly toil.

God bless such people today!
I pray for those I know personally
        and for the many unknown
        in like circumstances.
Sustain them by Your presence, Lord!

When the scaffolding falls

Shored up, Lord!
That's how my life has been,
held by a good steady scaffolding,
            supporting the whole.
Work was a solid scaffolding for many years.
My duties, my interests, my colleagues,
my comings and goings all regulated,
an even routine hemming me in
            yet supporting me
            in a not unpleasant way.
I knew who I was, where I was
            and what I was doing.

Marriage was a pleasing girder
            added to my life.
A comfortable support around me,
            complementing me.
It gave me someone to lean on
            until bereavement struck
            with shattering force.

Good health was a wonderful buttress
            to my activities.
To feel on top of things, to rejoice in doing,

revelling in a sense of achievement
      with almost unflagging energy.
Then sickness came and the pattern changed,
      my own strength seeped away.

The scaffoldings have fallen one by one
      and I have missed them, Lord.
Did I rely too much on them and too little on You?
I fear this is possible for now I feel exposed.
In my need I turn to You, Lord.
You are my strength and stay and You alone.
      Help me to believe it
and to live securely anchored in Your love.

Heaven must be vast

Heaven must be a vast place, Lord!
Myriads of souls from all corners of the earth
      made welcome by Your love
      for them as individuals.
It is beyond all human imagination . . .
Mrs Jones and Mrs Smith who attend the same church
      but never speak to each other
      will not easily be placed.
Their husbands, long time rivals,

are also likely to make sparks fly,
adding to the display of shooting stars.

Have You some sphere, Lord,
perhaps one of Your 'black holes' in space
where such contrary characters – millions of them –
    can cool off through the ages
      until they learn more sense?

Will theological controversy cease as we pass
    the heavenly threshold,
or shall we require barriers between the sects
    to keep the peace?
Shall we challenge Peter and Paul on aspects
    of their letters in Your book,
or listen to lectures as they defend their standpoints?

It is hopeless, Lord, to imagine Your heavenly realm.
    Forgive our human inability
    to comprehend Your master-mind.
You will find a way to accommodate us all
in the vast heaven prepared for Your children.

GOD AND MYSELF

My super-ego

Lord, my super-ego mocks me!
      He makes my life a misery
insisting on perfect performance all the time
      and taunting me when I fall short.
He lashes me with recriminations,
rubs salt into the tender wounds of my
      inflamed conscience
and makes my days a treadmill
      of unattainables.

Master, what shall I do with this super-ego?
      This idol of perfection
demands that I shall bow down and worship him,
suggesting that only by so doing can I be
      pleasing to You.
Is he the product of Satan's wiles?
      An over-enlarged Christian ideal

which dwarfs my possibilities and
      discourages me from trying.

I reject him! I smash this super-ego
      with his smug, complacent face
and perpetual self-righteous perfection.
Your love, Master, stretches out to faulty humans.
You remember that we are dust and You accept us
      as we are,
and train us gently into what we might be.
You give us courage to continue
      despite many setbacks.
My heart responds warmly to Your love.
Imperfect as I am I belong to You
      and would serve You.

The real me

Which is the real me, Master?
I ought to know myself for we have been linked
      for many years
but suddenly an accidental happening,
      some disappointment
      or unexpected news,
shows me to myself in another light

and I am glad – sometimes –
or appalled – most of the time –
      at what I find within.

Which is the real me, Lord?
Is there any 'real me' at all?
Am I like an onion covered
      in layer after layer,
        growing smaller and smaller
until the heart is reached?

You know me, Lord, right through
      all my protective skins.
I shudder when I think of all You know,
those things I can hide from others
who only see the outward stance.
In moments of intimate talk
      friends may glimpse another me,
but only Your eyes pierce to the centre.
      What do You find there?

Only You can bring integration, Master,
welding my being into wholeness,
an all-through genuineness of thought,
      act and will.
Do it for me, Lord!

Contortionist

Lord, I am a real contortionist!
I can tie myself into twisted knots
      with great speed and agility.
Knots from which I can't free myself
      nearly so rapidly.
I mean of course, Master, mental contortions,
      tangled reasoning, biased thinking,
assessing facts without full knowledge
      and arriving at false conclusions.

At times I find myself shackled and gagged
      by no one else than myself.
My mental processes churn on
      in the same old tracks
      round and round the subject
without seeing the openings which would cast
      new light on the matter.
Even when the path is clear
      I trip up over myself
      and land on my nose.

What makes me accident-prone
      in this sense, Master?

Is it some inward turmoil,
>some personal frustration,
which I haven't yet faced and conquered?
Please shed light on this problem.
>Help me to think clearly,
>to weigh matters calmly
and to arrive at right decisions with Your help.

God-flight

Lord, this instinct to avoid You,
>to hide away,
>seems universal,
but why should I seek to escape from You?
Is it because I fear You,
>or feel guilty
>or unworthy?

Where shall I hide when You are everywhere?
The top of Everest is as accessible to You
>as the deepest mine shaft.
The blare of my radio or TV can't drown
>Your voice within.
Locked doors and curtained windows do not
>keep You out.
Where can one hide?

The answer is *nowhere*!
Flight is not the solution to the problem.
      The true response is surrender.
God is not after me to punish me
      but to win me,
not to blame me but forgive me.
Why then should I seek to hide?

O God, take this fear of You from my heart . . .
Let me look up into Your face and say:
      Here I am, Lord,
      You've won!

Myself

How nice it would be, Master, to get away
      from myself!
To start a new life with another personality,
      a better one, of course.
Each morning when I view the same old face mirrored,
I know the old person is there within me.

I can change the exterior by a new hair style,
      new clothes . . .
I can alter the environment,

move house,
switch my job,
take a holiday abroad,
but the inner man remains the same.
I have to live with myself wherever I am.

It is obvious, Lord, that there is
only one solution
and that needs Your help.
You told us to love our neighbour *as ourself*
so I must start off by getting to like myself,
or else my neighbour would be badly treated.
What a lot You expect, Master!
To like what I know of myself needs vital changes
within me.
These only You can accomplish.
Let Your love, Master, overpower the self-hate within,
change my personality by a spiritual re-birth,
re-create me into a new person, Lord,
conformable to Your will
and much nicer to know.

Morbid scruples

It is good to have scruples, Master,
keen insight into the difference between
      right and wrong,
firm standards to uphold in matters small and great.
Morbid scruples, though, are different.
They are acquired sensitivities, often reactions
      from our growing years,
instilled into us dogmatically
      or imbibed indirectly.

Lord, You must shake Your head in despair
      at times,
when we make so much of so little.
If we had a photo of You from Your days on earth,
many people would insist on the same hair style
      and the same type of clothes.
However did we get to the point
where one sect regards a hair parting as worldly,
and another group allows a middle parting only?
Such teaching creates morbid scruples,
artificial standards of dress or conduct,
to flaunt which brings condemnation.

Free me, Lord, from morbid scruples.
Let me shun unhealthy introspection,
        break away from such fetters
and launch into the liberty of Your presence,
bathed in Your generous, forgiving love.

Temptation

Master, it is encouraging to learn
        that You too were tempted
        during Your years on earth.
Had You not had that experience I might come to You
        with less hope of being understood.
Temptation seems so *soiling*, Lord!
It leaves a stigma on the spirit,
        a smirch in the mind,
        a sense of unworthiness
        and of being unclean.
None of this can be true, Master,
since You were tempted yet without sin.

Here is my problem, Lord.
How can I distinguish between being tempted
and myself plotting some wrongdoing?

Both seem to start in the mind with stray thoughts
   forming into plans.
At what moment can I recognise and reject them?
Would that I had a sentinel on guard
   who would sound the alarm
when spiritual danger was near.
I have, Lord! I realise that Your spirit
will warn me of approaching evil
if I yield myself under Your control.
Thank You for that! And help me, Lord,
not to be downcast when tempted,
for it is part of spiritual growing
   towards maturity.

God-bathed

Today I rejoice, Master,
I glory in You and in Your love.
It bathes my soul with golden warmth;
   it quickens my pulse
   and lightens my step.
Praise be to Your holy Name!

This is an inward suffusion of God-presence.
Outside the world is cold and grey,

the sun hidden behind thick clouds.
The garden wilts under frost crystals,
    trees stand stark and grim,
yet in my heart, Lord, there is this glow
    of glory,
    this feeling of union,
    of acceptance,
    of receiving vital strength
straight from Your heart to mine,
    O Sun of my soul.

I feel God-bathed!
And as the solar sun invigorates my body
so does this contact with You brace
    and strengthen my spirit.
Would I could always live in this heavenly rapture,
receptive to Your action on my life.
    The spiritual glow will fade
but my soul is left re-invigorated,
replenished and *alive*.
    Thank you, Lord.

Debit or credit?

How does my account stand with You, Master?
      Is it in the red or black?
Of course I am reasoning on
      a purely commercial basis.
If I had been as long in a firm's employ
      as I have served You,
I should long ago have been retired
      with a golden handshake
      and a pension.

But Lord, I haven't sensed any suggestion
      from Your side
that I should retire from Your service!
You expect me to continue to life's end.
Instead of a golden handshake now,
have I to wait for a golden crown in glory?

This is just in fun, Lord.
      I'm glad You realise that.
I know full well that what You give me
      of pardon, inward joy and peace,
far exceeds anything I commit to You.
Your love overwhelms me,

sinks my small efforts to serve You
       to insignificance.
I am an unworthy servant . . .
You are a loving, living, generous God.
       Praise be to Your Name!
I'm eternally in debt to You.

Indwelling

You indwell us, Master . . .
What do You get out of that?
       A lot of problems
       a lot of heartache . . .
It is love's nature to want to be
       with the beloved.
'I in You' is the creature seeking the Creator
       of necessity
       for help and support.
'You in me' is divine condescension,
       a limiting beyond all belief.
I get the advantages, You the disadvantages.

Why do You do it, Lord?
       I know the answer.
You do it because of Your great love,

Your overwhelming compassion.
Your recorded incarnation in human flesh
        is repeated daily
as by Your spirit You indwell us today.
But at what cost to Yourself!
You meet choked channels of expression,
        narrow views and prejudices,
        lack of courage, faith and joy.
These are the bonds with which we bind You,
        free Spirit of the eternal God.
Forgive us that when we ask You to indwell us,
        we are such poor hosts.
Blaze Your way into our hearts, Lord,
        burning away the hindrances,
expanding us even beyond our own desires;
creating the climate where You can express Yourself
        through our feeble humanity.
        Do it now, Lord!

Spare parts

Are there spare parts for the spiritual life, Lord?
When faith in God's love has worn thin
        when trust in God is shattered,

when the lamp of hope flickers faintly . . .
Are spare parts available, Master?

Can living saints be donors to needy sinners?
      Offering a tender conscience
      a responsible mood
      a prayerful acceptance
      a strongly-built faith
out of their spiritual abundance?

I ponder these questions before You, Master,
and it seems to me that the answer is *yes*!
There *are* spare parts for the spiritual life
proffered through Your abounding mercy
      poured out in rich streams
      from the treasury of Your grace,
      and only awaiting acceptance.
And saints can be donors to modern prodigals
      through earnest, believing prayer,
through humbly and joyfully witnessing to what
      God has done for them.

So no one need despair,
however blank their present experience,
however low their spiritual temperature,
however hopelessly they regard themselves.
      Spare parts are available!
      Praise God for that!

Shake off the old broken scraps of faith,
tone up the soul's sagging muscles.
Brace your will for a new commitment.
     Ask your Maker for what you lack
and stride forward bravely.

GOD IN MY STRIVINGS

Tides

There is ebb and flow in spiritual tides, Lord,
for we are not always at our best.
There is despair in the ebb
when the sand wastes are revealed
      and rocks loom dangerously near.
Fears suck courage away
as a weight of loneliness crushes the soul
      and prayers die on the lips.

But there comes the turn of the tide,
      a flicker of hope
      a clutch at faith
      a whispered prayer.
The creeping waves of the incoming spiritual tide
      fill up the empty creek,
      with movement, sound and hope.
Then once again comes the full flood of the Spirit,

the soul soars in vibrant faith, words of praise
        pouring from the mouth
and joy filling the heart.

Must it be so, Master?
        Ebb and flood
        much and little
        gloom and glory
        comfort and despair?
Our very humanity creates this rhythm
        but *You are stable*!
Thank You, Lord.

Soul and body

Lord, what a strange double nature I have!
Am I a body hosting a soul
        as an honoured guest,
or a soul imprisoned in a body
        and longing for freedom?
Part of myself – my body – is perishable
        yet it is the part I know best;
the only part of me that I can see
        and recognise as myself.

That shadowy thing within me —
      call it soul or spirit,
is the undying part that will live on
      beyond the grave,
      the real me . . .
yet I hardly know it, Lord.

      It is Your law, Master,
that soul shall be housed in body throughout life.
Not like a kernel in a nutshell,
      loosely rolling round,
but joined by many invisible bonds,
interacting the one upon the other.
I can starve my soul while feeding my body
or enrich my soul while denying my body.
Help me to strike a right balance, Master, so that both
      can enjoy Your blessing;
the good health of the body becoming
      a potent vehicle for the soul,
the soul's harmony spilling peace into the nerves
and muscles as long as life shall last.

Sweets or stones?

Lord, words from Your Book are pleasant on the
tongue,
      like sweetmeats to savour slowly
      sucking out the nourishment,
enjoying the flavour and imbibing the goodness.
A humdrum day can be enhanced by the accompani-
ment
      of such wisdom.
A printed pearl of truth seized in the morning
can become a lasting meal for heart and mind
      during the long and heavy hours.
This I have known, Master, and I thank You.

Why then, Lord, are there other days . . .
      days when Your Word seems blank,
carrying no message to inspire me, no special pointer
      to meet my need?
Why should a text suddenly lose all meaning
      for me personally,
leaving me cold and unmoved,
the word feeling like a stone pushed uselessly
      around in my mouth
until I can get rid of it?

The difference can't be in the printed word!
It must be in my attitude to it
      and to You!
Days when I am close to You and You to me
are times when Your Word becomes alive,
      sparkling and invigorating,
      inspiring and sustaining.
Would that it were always so!
That is my prayer and longing today, Lord.

A new day

A new day has dawned!
Master, I want it to be a day
      spent with You.
As I drew back the curtains
      I lifted my heart to You,
asking Your blessing upon the hours ahead
and committing myself once more
      into Your care.

What a difference such a beginning makes
      even to the most humdrum day.
The moment of prayer is an act of worship,
      a linking on to You, Lord,

a step of faith before the unknown ahead.
Remembrance of that act of dedication
        casts a warm glow over duties
and tightens up any spiritual slackness.

Can any period of twelve hours
        be a *new* day?
Isn't today much like yesterday?
        It need not be.
Each dawn brings new possibilities,
        new challenges
        new evaluations,
if only I am alert enough to see them.
So let me brace my spirit by saying:
        'This is a new day;
it can be a good day with Your help, Lord.'

Translations

Master, You learned to speak at Your mother's knee
in the ordinary language of the day,
yet Your words come down to us through
        the pages of Your Book
in many different translations.

Translations which are quarrelled over,
      compared and disputed
      admired or criticised,
      accepted or rejected,
with one crying 'I am for Ancient'
and the other countering: 'and I for Modern'.

We have lost the sounds You spoke, Lord.
The soft winds of Palestine bore them away
      but the meaning lived on
in the hearts of those You chose to be with You.
We are now so far off in time that we are
      dependent on translators
to mediate Your message to us.

O Jesus Christ! Help us to grasp Your message
even if the frailty of human transmission
shows faults in the actual phrase-making.
You translated God to us by Your life
      and Your death.
You translated the Divine Search into human terms
and showed what life might be
      permeated by Your Spirit
and lived under God's control.
Let my heart be open to Your message
through whatever medium it comes.

Miniature Christians

Miniatures are popular, Master,
particularly in the gardening world
but hardly, I think, in Your realm.
  Dwarf plants are cultivated,
roots are severed, nourishment restrained,
anti-growth mixtures applied and for what?
  To produce a miniature tree
to stand in a pot on the coffee table.

If You, Lord, are not eager for dwarf Christians,
the Evil One is intent on their propagation.
He encourages a little religion, an outward show,
  oh! nothing extravagant of course,
just sufficient to produce a miniature Christian
  with stunted growth,
no depth of root into Your truths,
merely a shallow show of outward conformity.

You want virile, dedicated, all-out followers,
  trees of righteousness
standing strong, free and unbending
  against evil attacks
or the dangerous drought of an indifferent world.

Drop Your spiritual fertilisers into our souls, Lord,
      expanding the spread of our branches,
      speeding our searching roots,
making us trees of the Lord, full of vitality,
      living witnesses to Your power.

Winning others

Master, I should like to have a long talk with You
      about this subject,
for You know best all that is involved.
Many of us long to win souls for You.
From the standpoint of youth it seemed
      a challenging and concrete cause –
getting others to accept You
      as Saviour and Lord.

Master, how do You regard Your mission on earth?
You loved with supreme love,
      You died to save us
yet You were betrayed, deserted and crucified.
The net result of Your arduous campaigning
      for the Kingdom of God
was a handful of muscular fishermen
      and some devoted women,

but from that unpromising beginning
    sprang the Christian church.

Are we too hurried, too impatient
in wanting to get results for our labours?
To see the corn ripening in the fields
    we have only just sown?
To count the sheaves and enter the statistics?
Teach us, Master, that winning others is slow work
    and each small step is vital.
A handshake, a smile, a word, a prayer,
    a text from Your Book,
strengthening this one's faith, sharing some sorrow,
building up the Kingdom brick by brick,
not erecting a pre-fab ordered complete,
but working slowly for eternal gains.

An unlit candle

Like an unlit candle!
That's how I feel today, Master.
    The scene is set,
      the possibilities are there
but I need a spark to set me alight.

A candle can't light itself.
It is a helpless, lonely object,
a parody of what it might be until touched
      by a flickering match,
       a glowing taper
       or a flash of fire.
Then the candle lives and shines,
      fulfilling its mission,
serenely beautiful in its usefulness.

Lord, I need Your divine spark to light
      the candle of my heart today;
to create a flame that will burn and throb
      and bring to life
that which seems dead within me for the moment.
I stand, Lord, mute and helpless
      as an unlit candle,
awaiting the touch of Your fire
      to set me ablaze.
Do it now, Lord! Do it now!

A way of escape

Chore after chore until I am weary . . .
Is that all that life holds, Master?
A long line of tasks stretching out
      into the known future
and much further . . . into the space
of the unknown rest of my days.
However, You remind me that there are ways of escape
      without neglecting duty.

Memory is a way of escape while hands are busy
      with monotonous movements.
Thoughts can flash to happy scenes in the past.
Planning for the future can be a way of escape.
      Glowing dreams of what might be
speed away the hours and quotas are achieved.

Praying is a way of escape, making a tedious job
      into an offering to You, Lord.
You, who on earth toiled at a carpenter's bench
      with familiar tools
      held in competent hands.
You were preparing Yourself
      for Your redemptive mission,

while the sawdust drifted down
to coat the floor in fragrant softness.

At least I can lift my heart to You and ask
for courage to continue
for faith to hold fast
for peace of mind . . .
and that will be a way of escape
from dull montony
into a joyous moment of contact with You.

After the storm

Yesterday, Lord, it stormed all day!
Dark skies, slashing rain,
fierce winds and floods.
The world of nature seemed in chaos
and my heart trembled.

Today is quite different, Master.
The sun shines, the skies are clear
and chubby white clouds drift dreamily
across the pale blue heavens.
How my heart rejoices!

Storms come . . . and storms pass.
That is the lesson I must learn afresh.
It is good that I am reminded of it
     for life has other storms . . .
sudden crises, accidents and disasters,
     disillusions and disappointments.
These crush my heart with fear as they pound out
     their message of doom.
Yet they too will pass
     and possibly be forgotten.

Calm my heart, Lord, in the midst of the storm.
Say to me: 'Why are you afraid? Trust Me,
     I will help you through.'
Thank You, Master, for that word.

GOD FOR ALL
SEASONS

Begin again (New Year)

How many times, Lord, must I make
      a new start?
How often must I confess to You
      that I have failed?
Failed in my Christian duty,
     in my relationships
     in my prayer life
through inertia, busyness or apathy.

What a quagmire of undesirable traits
     mushed up together
     in an unsavoury bog
that clogs my footsteps on the Christian way!
You must be tired of listening
     to the dreary catalogue
     of my shortcomings,
just as I am tired of confessing them.

And yet something within me urges:
>try once more!
>Begin again!
I believe, Lord, it is Your voice in my heart,
>Your Spirit within me
that lights a faint glimmer of hope
>in the depressing darkness.

Dare I make a new start? I hesitate . . .
>reflect . . .
glimpse the abyss of despair yawning at my feet.
I clench my will to action as I say:
>'I'll try, Lord!'
'I throw myself upon Your mercy and by Your grace
I'll begin again. So help me God.'

The garlanded cross (Good Friday)

The wayside crucifix stood high, its foot
>deeply planted among heavy stones.
I had to raise my head to glimpse
the twisted features of the suffering Christ.
>The sculptor had been lavish

in his portrayal of blood from wounds
    in hands, feet and side.
I stood in silence, remembering, worshipping,
    before I turned away.

A coachload of tourists passed me
    in hilarious mood,
    singing and shouting.
A mocking cheer greeted the crucified Christ.
From the open windows some threw paper streamers
    at the figure on the cross,
garlanding it with multi-coloured bands
which fluttered in the breeze.
    Someone protested angrily
and the driver drew up to allow a man to descend.
He tried to climb the cross but it was too high,
so he had to leave the wind to strip it
    of its gaudy trimmings.

With revulsion in my heart, Lord,
    I tried to pray,
but all I could say was the echo
of Your words, Master, from Calvary:
'Father, forgive them, for they know not
    what they do.'

My living Lord (Easter)

Master, I believe in Your resurrection!
　　　You are my living Lord!
My mind tries to recapture the scene . . .

Slow dawning . . .
with the chill of night still present.
Shrouded forms of women steal silently along,
　　　going where?
To the tomb . . . to weep.
Heavy their hearts, laboured their breathing,
　　　slow their steps.

Daylight!
A clutch of fear at their hearts,
　　　a gasp of awe
　　　at the stone back-rolled,
　　　the tomb empty!

O panting hesitation . . .
　　　O growing expectation . . .
a glimpse, a shout, a stab of joy.
'He is not here. He is risen!'
　　　Waves of ecstasy.

It is as He said:
>He is not dead but risen.
Alive! My Lord is alive!

Full of what? (Whitsun)

Lord, I have been meditating . . .
The full vessel runs over with its own contents:
the selfish life drips selfishness,
the loving person spreads love around,
the careless man communicates
>a careless attitude,
heedless of others' feelings, needs or problems.

Lord, I want the overflow from my life
>to be good, helpful and kind.
I pray that what flows out from me
might represent You and not myself.
I know that only what is within can spill over.
No amount of juggling will enable
>a cup full of water
>to drip milk.
And no number of holy phrases
>and cited texts
will pour forth blessing and cheer

if the heart is full of its own goodness
       and not Yours.

Fill me, Lord, with Your Spirit,
so that I have enough for myself
and can overflow into other lives with Your love,
       courage, faith and power;
not consciously by my own act
       but by being used by You
as an irrigation channel to parched souls.

Good and bad (Harvest)

Life is a series of sowings and reapings.
This is what the years have taught me, Lord.
There are good harvests, bringing joy
       and fulfilment,
but there are also bad ones with their toll
       of heart-ache and disappointment.

We cast the seeds of acts and words
       so thoughtlessly and lightly,
forgetting that each will germinate, grow
       and bear its own crop.
We are baffled when we reap trouble and discord,

not realising that we ourselves planted the seeds.
Sometimes, though, to our utter surprise
      some happy events
      reveal their origin
in a few kindly words we spoke
or a friendly deed we did and then forgot.

Harvesting! It is Your law, Master:
      what we sow
      we inevitably reap,
whether we remember the sowing or not.
Help us then, dear Lord, to be watchful
      over our acts, our words
      and even our thoughts,
for they too bring a harvest of good or evil.

What's the date?
(Christmas)

You made quite a local impact, Master,
when as a babe You joined the human race
      in Bethlehem.
Wondrous tales abound of stars, angels,
      shepherds and wise men
all accompanying Your advent.

Many people do not believe that story.
They scoff at the Christmas gospel while enjoying
      Christmas festivities.
But while they scoff, they acknowledge You,
      You who they say never existed.
Every time they say: 'What's the date?'
      they are asking:
      'When was Jesus born?'
Each time they date a letter, they pay silent homage
      to Your coming.
Before Christ and After Christ . . .
      so is history divided.
BC and AD – Anno Domini – Year of our Lord.

Master, I pray at this festive season that someone
      who has lived quite factually
      'before Christ' in their lives
will take the personal decisive step into AD,
      year of our Lord,
acknowledging You as Saviour and King.

A new diary (Year's end)

What have I written, Lord, in my diary
      for the past twelve months?
Dare I open the book to see?
As I turn the pages I find with surprise
      that many are blank!
Days when I did nothing except . . .
      pass the hours
      in monotonous routine.
Nothing outstanding in thought or deed,
      nothing worth recording.

Other pages are badly blotted.
I was trying to achieve some goal,
      perhaps set by others
      or of my own choosing.
I tried and failed . . . and tried again,
      then gave up in disgust.
A few of the pages are heavily altered
      with many deletions.
Strong reactions to persons or circumstances,
      hot, rebellious days
When I scythed my way through opposition.

The year is at an end and the book is finished.
Not one entry can I now change, Master.
Tomorrow I open a new diary, its pages
      invitingly clean.
I stiffen my will with firm determination.
Help me, Lord, to live the new year worthily.

GOD AND MY PROBLEMS

Life's key

Master, is there a key to life?
A master key to unlock the mysteries,
to show how the balance is struck
and assure us that all will be finally well
       despite today's blows?
Is there a key to suffering,
       to sickness
       to unemployment,
to thwarted hopes and marital breakdowns,
       to death itself?

With the passing of time some things
       become clearer, Lord.
I see more plainly the linking
       of cause and effect,
the penalties that follow the breaking
       of natural laws,

which are Your laws,
the outworking of strained relationships,
widening small rifts into yawning chasms.

And yet, Lord, there remains so much
        that is veiled from us . . .
a piece of the puzzle that You hold
        in Your closed hand,
and about which we can only guess.
One day You will call us to Your side
        and doubtless reveal to us
the key that unlocks life's secrets.
Until then, Master, knowing You rule in love
we leave our unsolved problems in Your hands.

Guidance

Master, if I could see the future I would know
        how to act today.
I have never been tempted to read my horoscope
        in the daily press
or consult a fortune teller in her curtained booth,
yet I should like to glimpse a little
        of what the future holds.

You do well, though, to screen it from our gaze
lest we lose heart or become careless.

Lord, You watch over us all,
not with the quick eye of a naturalist
      observing an ant-heap,
but with a Father's love and care for us
      as individuals.
You know what lies before me
      and You can guide me
      step by step
if I give You the chance of so doing.

Help me, Master, to live so attuned to You,
      so responsive to You,
that I shall be guided into right paths
      one day at a time,
though the total future is veiled.
Let Your Spirit maintain an inward and
      loving compulsion,
holding me back from wrong paths and gently urging
      into the right way.
      I need Your guidance, Lord,
for life is a labyrinth difficult to negotiate
      on my own.

Self-reproach

Master, is self-reproach an angel
      or a bogey?
Is it Your pressure on a soul
or a ploy of the devil to harass Christians?
Is it a catharsis of the spirit
      or a drug?

From my own experience, Lord,
I take a negative view of it.
Self-reproach has battered and humiliated me
more times than it has led to betterment.
It has manacled me to my worst moments,
      saying spitefully:
'There! that is how you are!'
It has been a cloud on my horizon
      blotting out the sun,
a hindrance to my activity
      when I wished to serve You.

Self-examination has its occasional use,
but searching one's conscience is a dangerous game
      for a sensitive person to play.

Faults and weaknesses can be magnified,
      distorted beyond all reason,
and lead to blackness and despair.
Master, You never flayed any sinner with reproaches
      without giving a message of hope,
      of forgiveness,
      of restoration of relationship.
Self-reproach shuts me away from You,
      turns my eyes upon myself
and is therefore worse than useless.
      Let me shun it!

Facing both ways

Life is difficult, Master.
There seem to be two sides to every question,
      differing paths to each goal
and I am caught in the middle
      facing both ways.
There is the tug between body and soul
      action and prayer
      material and spiritual values
      self-denial and self-fulfilment.
They are two sides of one reality,
and seemingly battling for supremacy

with me clamped in the centre,
my feelings oscillating between them.

Give me guidance, Lord, on how to balance my life,
        to use it to best advantage.
As I hesitate between alternatives,
        direct my thinking,
lead me to the right decision and help me
        to follow it through.
If I have Your approval it will be easier
        to bear criticism.

Make me strong against the self-doubt that arises,
the questionings: would it be wise?
        would it be misinterpreted?
If in a moment of insight I see my way,
let me follow it when the clouds descend
        and cold mists envelop me.
The momentary hesitation over, let me step forth
        in faith that You are leading me
        in the right way.

Too religious

Is it possible, Lord, to be too religious?
    Certainly not too *good*,
but too unbending on religious rules?
Too assiduous in following forms and ceremonies?
Too painstaking in adhering to a set programme
    of religious exercises?

Master, I am bombarding You with questions
    but they arise in my heart
and I feel I must ventilate them with You.
What started these thoughts was a whole day
    with Mr and Mrs B. Right.
They certainly walk a narrow path,
    not out in nature
    but in their attitudes.
This is allowed; that is proscribed;
this action accepted, that frowned upon.
They had it all worked out in detail.

I reacted strongly, Lord, against that way
    of living the Christian life.
It seemed just a series of taboos
    with little permitted

and less recommended.
I felt they were hemmed in with religious fences.
Somehow I was reminded of the Pharisees
      of Your time on earth.
Can it be that some of them are still around?

Loss or gain?

Master, Your Book speaks of sowing to reap,
      giving to get
      dying to live . . .
It seems there must be self-renunciation
      before there can be fulfilment.
There must be a period of persistent sowing
      in all weathers and hard conditions
      before any harvest can be reaped.
There must be open-handed giving before receiving.

My question today, Master, is:
which is the greater – loss or gain?
By acknowledging You as Lord and King
      do I lose more than I gain?
      Do I give more than I get?
Is my self-surrender just Your chance
      to make me miserable,

to limit me by restrictions,
or is it Your opportunity to bring me
    to fullest potential?

Thank You, Lord, that I know the answer!
The more I welcome Your indwelling, Your guidance,
    Your control,
the more integrated and radiant my life will be.
Your arms are laden with precious spiritual gifts
    if I will but receive them
by renouncing self and acknowledging You as Lord.
    My gain will be infinite . . .
    My loss . . .? Negligible!

Hurry!

Hurry! This is your last chance . . .
Hurry! Post the coupon now.
Hurry! Do it today!
Master, I am tired of hurrying,
weary of being urged to scamper faster,
not for any purpose of my own but merely
    to please advertisers.
It is their business, not mine.
They are placing burdens on me,

loading me with their chains
in order to make a sale,
of something I do not want or need.
I am tired of the eternal pace-setting
to keep up with other people
to equal them in activity
and outshine them in possessions.

You are never in a hurry, Lord.
Many times I wish that You were!
Your mills grind infinitely slowly . . .
You give me time to breathe, to consider,
You woo rather than force.
Your only pressure is a loving invitation
to accept what You offer,
forgiveness, reconcilation,
followed by joy and peace.

You point no shot-gun at my head
saying: 'Now or never'.
You are patient and long-suffering.
Your very love breaks me down
to the point of surrender.
Thank You for that, Lord.

Have mercy!

Have mercy, O Lord, upon us!
Look down in compassion upon this world
        that You have made,
beautiful but bestial, fair though foul,
        soulful but sinful.

Forgive us for what we have done
        with the good gifts You gave,
our thoughtless misuse of natural resources,
our careless scattering of rubbish,
        our litter-bug habits,
our promptness in using then discarding,
with so little ability to create.
        These are outward sins.

Most of all, dear Lord, forgive us
        our inward sins.
Greed for money or power,
for more food than is good for us,
        for excitement and pleasure
        for mistaking lust for love
        violence for adventure
and watching TV instead of personal involvement.

Forgive us our petty hatreds,
      our daily complaints,
the knife-edge of our injured pride,
      our bitter words and haughty mien.
These . . . and many more . . . are our inward sins.
Have mercy upon us, O Lord!
      Forgive us our sins!

Meanness

Today, Master, a question faces me.
As I cast my thoughts down the vista of the past,
what do I most regret in the years that have slipped
      so hastily away?
I wriggle under the query
      for it makes me uncomfortable,
      but You insist.

What do I most regret as I look back?
I swallow hard and confess:
I most regret the small meannesses
      of which I have been guilty . . .
the word of praise I didn't speak,
the loving gesture I didn't make,
the friendly letter I didn't write . . .

my cursed reticence,
my reluctance to show my deepest feelings,
which led me to miss so many chances
of cheering a fellow wanderer along life's way.

Am I too set, Lord, in older days
          to change my ways?
I fear so, yet within me pipes
          a trill of hope, saying:
'Time is still your friend. You can improve.'
So help me, Lord!
The past I cannot alter but from it
          I can learn.
From today I can do better, by Your aid.

The unwanted gift

It is some time since it happened, Lord,
          but it still smarts a bit.
          My gift was unwelcome.
Oh! it was quite a simple thing
but it had cost me some time to make
and I had hoped it would give pleasure.
Much later I found it put away in a cupboard,
          unused and unwanted.

My immediate reaction was to feel hurt.
Some of myself had gone into my gift.
Master, I began to feel badly disappointed,
  then suddenly I saw reason.
I had given my friend what I thought she would like
  without checking with her beforehand.
I had enjoyed planning and making it
  according to my own ideas
and naively expected her to be delighted.
I wanted both the pleasure of giving a gift
but also of being thanked and praised.

Sometimes, Lord, I wonder how You feel
  about our offerings to You.
We give a little time, money, service,
  feeling how generous we are
  and how pleased You must be.
Do You ever reject our gifts? I don't think so;
I believe You accept them warmly,
magnanimously overlooking their insignificance,
like a good father with his child.

GOD TEACHES ME

Human help

Lord, You must forgive me if I say
       I need human help.
You are the source of all grace and strength
but at times I crave for human aid.
An outstretched hand, a smile, a friendly word,
       a cheery phone call,
       an understanding letter,
encouragement from a fellow pilgrim.

It is an admission of weakness, Master.
       Of that I am sure.
You should be my All-in-all,
       sufficient for every need.
I should be able to live sustained only
       by my trust in You,
but my faith is often frail and then
       You seem so far away
       and even unreal.

Another thought impinges on my mind . . .
If I need the help of others, then surely
      they need mine.
This is a nudge from You, Lord,
turning me from my self-absorption to consider
      my neighbour's trials.
Human help I crave. Human help I must give.
Then Your earthly children will be linked
      by ties of caring,
      by bonds of compassion,
steadying the stumbling, urging each other forward,
smiling into another's eyes and saying:
      'Together, in God's strength.'

Ill-timed prayers

It was my mistake, Lord.
I thought that event was today and found
      it took place yesterday.
There was I praying for Your blessing
      on a past happening . . .
What do You do with such ill-timed prayers?
I cannot think, Master, that they are simply cast
      into Your heavenly waste-paper basket
      as useless lumber.

Surely in the divine economy
       You will be able to use them.

Do I imagine too much when I picture
       a heavenly conveyer belt
       ceaselessly moving forward,
carrying prayers, longings, desires,
       from the past into the future?
Into that stream of directed power
       my simple prayer must have fallen;
not availing much for the particular moment
       I had in mind
but becoming a tiny drop in the strengthening
       stream of grace
       flowing before Your throne
       for re-channelling earthwards.

I'm not worried then, about my mistimed prayers,
You will use them somehow, somewhere, Lord.

The accident that wasn't

My heart stood still
       as I watched, Master . . .
a lorry and a bus bent on a head-on crash.

I braced myself for the impact
     but nothing happened.
I blinked hard and realised I was watching
     one line of traffic
in a reflecting glass which distorted its direction.

But in the split second when I expected
     the noisy collision,
I had lifted my heart to You in prayer.
     For what I do not know
for I was not personally involved.
My instinct cried out: 'O God!' . . .
     a wordless plea for help.
Afterwards I could only say: 'Thank You'
for the accident that didn't happen.

How do people live who are sufficient for themselves,
who in a crisis have no one to turn to for help,
and no one to thank when danger is averted?
     Are they strong?
     Or foolish?
I am fortunate who know You, Lord,
     as one to whom I can turn
at all times and in all places,
in accidents that do happen
     and those that don't.

Bondage

Lord, I am not free!
I live in perpetual bondage to tradition,
      to tight schedules,
      to imposed priorities.
I am hemmed in by precedent and convention,
      hampered by prejudice . . .
and I rebel!

Some of these are necessary.
      That I accept, Master.
I am one in a team and I must play my part
      and accept my responsibilities.
But is my loyalty to the group greater than
      my devotion to You, Lord?
Is my concern for the success of our venture
      swayed by personal ambition,
      or zeal for Your Kingdom?

At times I feel a slave to duty,
working mechanically in well-defined ways
having bludgeoned my mind to only one thought –
      to keep going at full stretch.
I have made a fetish of duty –
      a swollen, unrealistic idol

which I can never satisfy.
Where is the freedom You promised, Lord?

All right! I accept Your rebuke –
      I will slow down . . .
A breath of Your deep calm quiets my heart;
instead of me working my fingers to the bone
      for You,
You will direct my energies into a controlled pattern,
allowing time for recreation, reading and fellowship.
Thus I shall become a better worker,
      with less risk of a breakdown.

Gluttony

Gluttony, Lord, is an ugly word,
      and it conjures up a bad image
of a fatty brandishing knife and fork
and gourmandising from heaped-up dishes.
Your Book reminds us that gluttony
      is one of the seven deadly sins,
but we hear very little about it otherwise.

You, Master, were called 'a glutton
      and a wine-bibber'.

That gives me something to think about.
    No one can escape
the poisoned barbs of criticism,
but they wing their way with deadlier aim
    tipped with a snippet of truth.
It is recorded that You graced many
    a laden table with Your presence.
You enjoyed festivities and special occasions,
and You certainly did not frown on them.

Yet Your everyday life was uncluttered and simple,
    as befitted a wandering Teacher.
At Your death Your only possession of value
    was a seamless tunic –
no doubt a gift, not a purchase.
Master, from You I must learn the delicate balance
between personal austerity and rejoicing with others
    at festive moments.
Even so, guard me from self-indulgence
    and the sin of gluttony.

Aggrieved

I'm feeling aggrieved, Lord, really put out,
    over a very small matter too.
I'm ashamed to admit, Master,

that it was just a change of TV programme
which no longer fitted my lunch hour.
I enjoyed watching and listening to it
  as I ate alone.
It was a company, it gave interest
  and *it was part of my day*.

So I feel peeved and disappointed.
  I never realised before
how much I relied on that programme
  to accompany my meal.
I could of course postpone my lunch
  a couple of hours,
but that would upset the rhythm of my day.

Lord, at the same time that I am annoyed,
  I am appalled . . .
appalled that so small a thing as a change
  of programme
can upset me to such a degree,
while the world shudders and writhes in wars,
  earthquakes and bombings.
It is nonsense that I should feel so deprived –
a momentary weakness that I must overcome.
  You will help me, Lord?
  I know You will.

Price tab

It gave me a real start, Master,
to see myself suddenly in the mirror
with a price tab hung round my neck.
Had I been walking round like that all morning?
      Shopping, chatting, bus-queueing
        with a white price ticket
dangling for all to see?

I moved and my reflection in the shop window moved.
      With a great sigh of relief
I realised that the price tab was left behind
      hanging on a wax model.
It was *her* price, not mine
      that was displayed.

It had given me a momentary shock, Master,
so unpleasant that I had not read
      the figure on the ticket.
What did *she* cost? What was *I* worth?
That question followed me all day.
If we all wore realistic price tabs of our worth
in terms of what we contribute to life,
      what eye-openers there would be!
Some very ordinary people would be highly priced,
while front-line figures might be half-price bargains.

What a good thing that we are not asked
      to set a price upon ourselves,
      or more to the point, on others.
Only You, Master, know our true worth
      and judge us accordingly.

Dark glasses

A marvellous invention, Master, tinted glasses
      to counteract eye strain.
You and Your followers knew nothing of that
      as you roamed round Galilee.
Perhaps Your eyes were stronger through less use
      of artificial light,
for an oil lamp gives such a gentle glow.
However, dark glasses are useful, Lord,
      to combat sun glare
and they also tone down unpleasant scenes.

I must beware, though, of wearing dark glasses
      on my soul's eyes.
It would be comforting . . . an easy way out,
not having to confront the full blaze of truth
      about myself,
or the hard facts of my short-comings.

Unpleasant matters would be toned down,
the shock-glare smoothed from certain acts,
a false green tinting added to dry growth . . .
O Master, it is so easy to be deceived!
Let me welcome the full penetrating light
      of Your gaze
however uncomfortable I feel, knowing that
only You can both diagnose and heal.
Spiritual dark glasses must be banned!

Man or machine?

Master, I am irritated . . .
      Modern life is so mechanical!
I phone for a repair man and
      a tape recorder answers me:
'Give your name, address and telephone number.
State your errand briefly and our agent
      will ring you later.'
It's inhuman!
Time and money saving, of course, to have a box
      on duty day and night,
but I want a human voice, a listening ear,
      an understanding person.
I don't want to air my need to a machine.

Still irritated, I think of You, Lord.
How we call on You at any time,
pressing our needs with urgent insistence,
        sure of Your kind attention.
Thank God there is no tape machine
        installed in heaven,
        recording our pleas
and promising that they will be dealt with
        in strict rotation.

My annoyance subsides as I meditate, Master,
firm in my belief that Your ear is open to my cry
        whenever I call on You.
I rest in Your loving care, not afraid of troubling You
        by my frequent requests.
You are there! And You are my God and Father.